Kids' Question & Answer Book

Compiled by Anna Pansini
Illustrated by Renzo Barto

Troll Associates

Library of Congress Cataloging-in-Publication Data

Pansini, Anna.
   Kids' question and answer book / compiled by Anna Pansini;
illustrated by Renzo Barto.
     p.   cm.
   Summary: Second and third graders answer their own questions about
health, nature, and science.
   ISBN 0-8167-2306-0 (lib. bdg.)   ISBN 0-8167-2307-9 (pbk.)
   1. Children's questions and answers. [1. Questions and answers.]
I. Pansini, Anna. II. Barto, Renzo, ill.
AG195.K43 1991
031.02—dc20   90-43969

If you are like most kids, you wonder about many things. You have plenty of questions, and you want answers to them—fast. So we challenged kids all across America to come up with the answers to the questions they wonder about most. The response was tremendous!

The very best questions and answers were compiled and put into this book, and two others—*"I Wonder Why"* and *Great Answer Book.* Each is filled with over 100 questions and answers on topics that kids are curious about.

Each contestant's name appears under the answers. Each book contains an alphabetical listing of winners, along with age or grade, school, and school address.

Finally, we'd like to thank all the students who entered the contest and the teachers who encouraged them.

I wonder why woodpeckers don't get headaches when they peck on trees...

Woodpeckers don't get headaches when they peck on trees because they have very hard bills and special padding in their heads.

Chris Dixon

I wonder why deer have antlers...

Antlers are used for defense. Antlers are bone growths from the heads of most male deer and some female deer. The only male deer without antlers are the Chinese water deer and the musk deer. The caribou and reindeer are the only deer in which both the male and female have antlers.

Nicole DelCorpo

I wonder how rabbits can hear sounds that are very far away...

Rabbits can move their long ears close together or move each one separately so that they can catch even very faint sounds from a very far distance.

Melissa McArthur

I wonder why snakes slither...

Slithering is the only way that most snakes can move because they don't have legs. It may look like snakes are moving fast but the fastest any snake has ever traveled is seven miles per hour.

Allison Gray

I wonder if bats are truly blind and cannot see in daylight...

No, actually bats are not blind and can see in daylight. Echolocation is a word used to describe some bats' way of using echoes to sense objects at night. As it flies at night, a bat repeatedly makes a noise, and sound waves bounce back. The vibrations go through a bat's ears and the eardrum vibrates, sending a message to its brain. The brain then tells the bat where and how far away objects are. So bats actually can see a little in daylight and use "radar" at night.

Fairreia Lindstrom

I wonder why polar bears are white...

- Polar bears are white so they can hide easily in the snow.

Paul Ondo

I wonder why elephants have big ears...

An elephant's big ears help it to keep cool. Some elephants live in Africa where the sun is very hot. To stay cool, they fan themselves with their big ears. They also stick out their ears to make themselves look fierce when they charge an enemy.

Not all elephants have big ears. The Indian elephant, which lives in shady forests, has smaller ears.

Matthew Kois

5

I wonder why birds have wings...

All birds have wings. There are all kinds and sizes of wings. I always thought wings were for flying, but some birds don't even fly. So why do they have wings?

Most birds do fly. They fly to get away from their enemies, and they fly to get their food.

An albatross has long, pointed wings because it has to glide for a long time to look for food. A chimney swift has narrow wings so it can catch flying insects. It has to move really fast. A pheasant eats seeds, berries, and insects on the ground, but it has broad, rounded wings so it can take off quickly when its enemies get close.

Some birds don't fly even though they have wings. Their food is on the ground, and they use their wings to protect themselves from their enemies. The penguins use their wings to swim fast in the water to trap fish. The ostrich uses his wings to keep his balance when he runs away from his enemies. The kiwi doesn't use its tiny wings at all.

Brooks Barber

I wonder why a rattlesnake's tail rattles...

The rattlesnake is poisonous, but it often gives a warning before it bites. On the end of its tail is a rattle made of dead scales. The rattle makes a whirring, buzzing sound when the snake shakes it, warning its enemies to stay away. Each time the rattlesnake grows a new skin, its rattle gets longer.

Joshua Douin

I wonder what jackrabbits are...

Jackrabbits aren't really rabbits at all. They are hares. Hares are bigger than rabbits and have longer ears and legs. They are born with their eyes open and with fur on their bodies. They weigh 6-12 pounds and live in open areas, scrubby deserts, and grassy plains. They are found in almost all areas of the midwestern and western states.

Kelly Callister

I wonder why animals hibernate for the winter...

There are many animals that hibernate for the winter. This means that they spend a long period of time asleep or in a deep rest. Squirrels, woodchucks and some other rodents hibernate so they can live through the cold weather when there is only a small amount of food for them to find. The animals that hibernate are warm-blooded.

When an animal hibernates, the temperature of its body goes down almost to freezing and its heartbeat and breathing slow down. This makes the animal not need much food and water. The animal stops moving and can live for a long time on its own fat. Animals get ready for hibernation by eating large amounts of food that turn into fat. They also look for a cave or dig a hole to protect themselves for their long sleep.

Daniel Rivera

I wonder why most animals are not purple or pink...

If most animals were purple or pink, they could easily be seen by their enemies. If rabbits or squirrels were pink, they would easily be seen by hunters or predators. The colors of many animals blend in with their surroundings. This keeps them from being shot or eaten.

Rachel Westphahl

I wonder why skunks have such a bad odor...

I think skunks are pretty animals, and I can't understand how this beautiful, furry animal could smell so bad. A skunk is also called a polecat. It is a member of the weasel family. There are different kinds of skunks, and they live all around North, Central, and South America. Some types of skunks are the hog-nosed skunk, hooded skunk, spotted skunk, and striped skunk. The striped skunk is mostly found in North America.

The skunk has a bad odor because that is its way of protecting itself. When the skunk feels danger coming, it sprays a bad scent toward the person or animal that is threatening it. The spray is a yellow liquid that can be smelled as far away as twelve feet. Skunks can be tamed as pets. Their scent glands can be used to make perfume.

Teressa Stringfield

7

I wonder how a camel can live in the desert without drinking water for a long time...

Most people think that camels store water in their humps, but scientists have told us this is not true. The humps are storage for fat. When the camel has nothing to eat, it gets energy from the stored fat and the humps get smaller. Camels must drink water but they can also get water in the desert from green plants they eat. Did you know that camels do not perspire unless it is very hot? They save their water inside their bodies so they will need less water.

Pamela Toth

I wonder if animals have the same five senses that people do...

Many animals have the same five senses that people have. Monkeys, horses, dogs, cats, and rabbits have eyes, ears and noses that work very much like ours. However, some of these sense organs are much more sensitive than ours. For example, dogs can hear very high-pitched sounds that humans can't hear. Dogs also have a better sense of smell than we do. Cats, owls, and raccoons can see at night when we cannot. Fish have a special organ called a lateral line, which helps them feel the movement of the water around them. It helps fish know if other water animals are around them.

Adam Wheeler

I wonder why hamsters store food in their cheeks...

Hamsters store food in their cheeks so they will have something to eat during the night. They also store food when they sleep through the winter.

Amy Mathews

I wonder why the dinosaurs became extinct...

Nobody knows why the dinosaurs became extinct, but scientists have some good theories. Some scientists think that a change in the climate killed the plant-eating dinosaurs by killing the plants they ate as food. Some think small animals ate the dinosaurs' eggs. Huge floods or volcanic eruptions could have killed plant and animal life. A large asteroid may have hit the earth, causing dust to block out the sun, killing plants and the animals that ate the plants. A comet shower or a star exploding nearby could also have killed the dinosaurs. As you can see, nobody knows what really happened to the dinosaurs.

Angel Stephens

I wonder why crickets make so much noise...

Usually only the male cricket makes noise. A cricket makes all that noise by rubbing his wings together. A cricket does not sing, he fiddles. The reason the male cricket fiddles so much is to make a female cricket come to him. In some countries, crickets are considered to bring luck, and people put crickets in special little boxes and bring them into their homes so they can hear the crickets' cheerful songs.

Julie Hunter

I wonder how insects breathe...

Insects have breathing pores or holes above and below their stomachs. They breathe in air through their breathing pores, which are called spiracles.

Aaron Seaman

I wonder why ants clean their antennas with their front legs...

They clean their antennas because they can touch, smell, and hear better with a clean antenna.

Stephen Engel

I wonder why spiders don't get caught in their own webs...

Spiders make different kinds of silk. One kind is a fine kind called the dragline. This is their safety line and always connects them to their web. Another kind is used to wrap up their prey. The spider uses several other kinds of silk to make its web. One kind is very firm, dry, and not sticky. Another is sticky and stretchy elastic. This is what traps the prey. The spider doesn't get stuck because it crawls on the dry silk threads. Another reason is that the spider's body is oily and won't stick to the sticky silk.

Michael Berry

I wonder why spiders spin webs...

Spiders spin webs in the air to catch insects so they can eat them.

Amy Gammon

I wonder why you never see baby butterflies...

You never see baby butterflies because butterflies hatch from their cocoons when they are full adults. When butterflies are babies, they are caterpillars.

Jessica Carter

I wonder why it itches when a mosquito bites...

Only the female mosquito bites. Mosquitoes don't really bite because they cannot open their jaws. When a mosquito bites, she stabs your skin with the needlelike parts of her mouth, called stylets. Then she puts her saliva into your skin. The saliva keeps your blood flowing so the mosquito can sip it more easily. Most people are allergic to the mosquito's saliva. That's why you get a little bump on your skin that itches when a mosquito bites you.

Jacob Hall

10

I wonder why dogs have wet noses...

Moisture on a dog's nose helps it detect odors. It comes from a gland inside the nose.

Heather Grosserode

I wonder why people say black cats are unlucky...

In the Middle Ages, people believed that witches could turn into cats. Some people say black cats are unlucky because they associate them with witches.

Andrea Rerea Vanerelli

I wonder why cats' eyes glow in the dark...

Cats have a special part of their eye that acts like a mirror. At night, dim light bounces off this special part inside the eye to help the cat see.

Edward Overton

I wonder why cats have whiskers...

Cats cannot see in total darkness. The whiskers of a cat are special hairs that are very sensitive to touch. These hairs are called "tactile hairs." They grow on the chin, at the sides of the face, and above the eyes. The whiskers brush against objects and help a cat to know which way to go in the dark.

Rosanna Gahhos

I wonder what makes Siamese cats different from other cats...

The main difference is the way they look. All Siamese cats have blue eyes. Sometimes their eyes are crossed. When they are born, they are white. When they get bigger, they become creamy colored yellow (or another light color) and they develop brown, red, or blue spots called points. The points are on their feet, legs, ears, tail, and face. Siamese cats come from Thailand, which used to be called Siam. They are very clean. They are like dogs in some ways—they can walk on a leash and even fetch. Their voices sound different from other cats'—their meows can sound like a human baby.

Jessica Toth

I wonder why cats like milk...

Some cats like milk because it is good for their bodies, and they like the taste. Cats also like cream and other dairy products like butter and cottage cheese. Cats also need to drink fresh water, not just milk. Some people think that cats can get all their nourishment from milk alone, but cats need many different kinds of food. They like fish, beef, kidney, heart, and chopped liver. I think this sounds very yucky. Could this be why they like milk so much? Mother cats drink milk to help nurse their kittens. Cats should drink lots at this time. Kittens love their mother's milk best!

Ashley Mutter

I wonder why cats have tails...

Cats have tails to help them keep balance. When a cat falls, it swings its tail and twists its body so it will land on its feet.

Becky Bricker

I wonder why cats have pads on their feet...

The pads on cats' feet help them move silently when they hunt other animals. They move up to their prey very slowly and then they pounce on it. Cats also have sharp teeth and claws to help them catch their prey. They have rough tongues to help them remove pieces of meat from bones. They can pull in their claws when they do not need to use them. Cats do most of their hunting at night. Their pupils open wide so they can see better in the dark. Cats have long whiskers that are used as feelers. Cats' ears are very good. It is almost impossible to sneak up on a cat. Some people have silly ideas about cats—they think that cats have nine lives when they really only have one.

Nicky Demarchi

I wonder why cats rub up against you when they see you...

The reason cats rub up against you when they see you is partly to be friendly with you. But there is more to it than that. The cat usually starts by pressing against you with the top of its head or the side of its face, then rubs all along its body and finally may wrap its tail around you. There are special scent glands on the cat's temples and around its mouth and tail. Without you even realizing it, the cat has given you its special scent.

Lindsay Sawyer

I wonder why cats purr...

Cats purr when they are well-fed or happy. When they are sick or in pain, they have a special purr.

There is a legend about how a cat got its purr. It is a French tale. A beautiful princess had to spin 10,000 balls of linen in only a month, or her prince would die! She had three clever cats; they spun the fiber into threads for her on spinning wheels. Their hard work saved the prince! The cats were honored at the wedding feast. They curled up and began humming—just like spinning wheels. The purr was a gift to them for helping the princess. That's why cats purr.

My cats, Ping and Pistachio, are champion purrers!

Stephen Ricks

I wonder why dogs wag their tails...

Dogs wag their tails when they are happy, excited, mad or angry. They also wag their tails when they want to go in, go out, or just want to play with you. They might wag their tails to wave at you, or maybe they want a bone. I wonder what would happen if they wagged their tails very swiftly—would they fly high into the sky?

Brooke Pantano

I wonder why dogs scratch so much...

A dog scratches itself when it has fleas, or it might still have some soap on its body from when it was washed, or it may need to be washed, or it may have ticks, which it could have gotten when it was outside with other dogs.

Christy Meyer

I wonder how the Great Lakes formed...

Thousands of years ago, glaciers covered the northern parts of North America. The glaciers dug out lots of earth and rock. When the glaciers melted during the Ice Age, these deep holes became filled with water.

Katie Garstecki

I wonder why there are different tides...

Ocean tides are caused by the pull of the sun and the moon on the earth. When the moon is close to a certain part of the earth, that area has high tides. When we have a full moon or new moon, we have very high tides called spring tides. At other times, the pull of the sun and the moon work against each other and the tides are lower. I like high tides because the fish come close to the shore.

Jake Dean

I wonder where the ocean is the deepest...

The deepest spot of the ocean is the Mariana Trench in the Pacific Ocean. This spot is near the Mariana Islands, southwest of Guam. The water there is over 36,000 feet deep—or nearly 7 miles from the surface to the bottom. This is deep enough to cover the highest mountain in the world—Mount Everest—which is nearly 6 miles high.

Shauntelle Lake

I wonder how you can tell the difference between a frog and a toad...

It is not easy to tell a frog and a toad apart. They are both amphibians. Most frogs and toads are born in the water like fish, and are called tadpoles. Then they grow legs and lungs and live on the land. Most frogs stay near the water, while toads live more inland. The biggest difference between a frog and a toad is that frogs have moist, smooth skin and toads have dry, bumpy skin. Another way to tell them apart is by looking at their back legs. A frog's back legs are long and powerful and the toad's legs are much shorter. I have a pet frog named Abraham who lives under my back porch.

Krystal Anderson

I wonder why frogs don't have ears...

Frogs don't have ears that stick out of their heads. They have eardrums that are big circles behind the frog's eyes. Sound from the air or water causes the eardrum to vibrate. Then the frog can hear.

Ben Kankey

I wonder why the sea is blue...

The sea looks blue because of the way sunlight is scattered on the water. Light rays are reflected by the sea. When sunlight shines on sea water, the yellow, orange, and red rays fade first. The blue light rays get scattered best. Since the blue is scattered best, our eyes tell us the sea is blue.

Sally Richardson

I wonder why the ocean is salty...

Some of the salt in the ocean is from the land. When it rains, the flowing water picks up some salt and carries it to the rivers. Then the rivers carry the salt to the ocean. But we do not know how salt first got in the ocean.

Eric Whidden

I wonder why ducks don't get wet...

Ducks have an oil gland near their tail. They use their beaks to wipe the oil on their feathers. That is called preening. Oil and water don't mix. Since their feathers are covered with oil, the water rolls right off the feathers, so the ducks don't get wet.

Sean Godfrey

I wonder where seashells come from...

There are more than 65,000 kinds of mollusks. Next to insects, they are the largest category of animals in the world. Many of the mollusks live in the sea. When the mollusks grow, many grow shells to protect them from animals that might eat them. When they die, their shells are left behind. The shells float around in the sea until they wash up on the beach as seashells.

Marianne Shaffer

I wonder how fish get clean...

There are special fish that act like cleaners. Some people call them "doctor fish" but their real name is wrasse. Wrasses help keep many other fish healthy and clean. Wrasses go into the mouths of other fish and remove pests, leftover food, bacteria and dead skin. For doing this cleaning job, they are rewarded with being able to eat the things they pick off. They think it's a free supper. This is one way fish get clean.

Meredith Beattie

I wonder why snails are so slow...

It's because they have only one foot. The muscles in this foot tighten to make it move.

Jerod Weiss

I wonder how starfish eat...

The starfish uses its feet to open a clam's shell, then pushes its stomach onto the shell to absorb the clam.

James Merriman

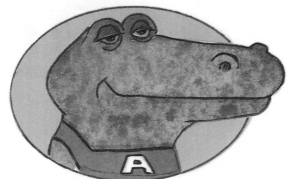 

I wonder what is the difference between crocodiles and alligators...

A crocodile has a long, narrow nose while an alligator's nose is short and wide. You can see some of a crocodile's teeth when it shuts its mouth, but when an alligator shuts its mouth, you cannot see any teeth. A crocodile is longer than an alligator.

Jenny Higham

I wonder how frogs breathe in water...

Frogs can breathe through their skin or through their lungs. In water, the oxygen in the water goes right through their skin and into their blood, so frogs can stay in water for a long time without having to come up for air. On land, they can breathe through their lungs like humans.

David Butler

I wonder how sharks breathe in water...

Water enters the shark's mouth and leaves through the gills. The gills filter the oxygen out as the water passes through. That is how sharks get oxygen underwater.

Nicole DeWilfond

I wonder why it rains...

Rain comes from big clouds, little clouds, black clouds, and gray clouds. Rain may come from clouds all over the sky. Clouds are made of little drops of water called droplets. Droplets are so small that you cannot see them. The droplets make a little cloud. Water evaporates from lakes and rivers, from trees and grass and from the ground. Water evaporates and makes water vapor, which is carried by the air into the sky. The higher it goes, the colder it gets, and the vapor turns into water droplets, which turn to clouds.

Sarah Marin

I wonder why hurricanes have names...

We give hurricanes names to keep them straight. If we didn't call them names, people would get confused as to which hurricane they were talking about.

Robin Schroer

I wonder why fog covers the ground...

Fog is a cloud that forms so low that it lies near the surface of the ground or the surface of a body of water. Fog forms when the wind blows warm moist air over a cold surface.

Fog mostly forms during the night. It leaves the grass wet. You don't feel it, but you know it's there because you can see it. The fog doesn't last all day because it lifts and goes away. Then we can see the land again.

Jennifer Mata

18

I wonder why it thunders...

Lightning causes thunder. When the lightning flashes through the air, the temperature of the air heats up. The hot air expands and bangs into cooler air nearby. The moving air creates sound waves that rush away from the lightning flash. When the sound waves reach your ears, you hear thunder.

Tiffany Bowman

I wonder why clouds move...

Air pushes the clouds, which causes them to move. If there was no air, the clouds would always stay in the same place. But if they never moved, rain or snow would always come down in the same place. So we need air to move the clouds from place to place.

Marianne Jennings

I wonder why raindrops look blue...

Raindrops look blue because of the sky's reflection in them.

Beth Indra

I wonder why it rains...

My friend thinks it rains so we will have water to drink. My sister thinks it rains so the grass and trees will grow. Daddy thinks it rains so the lakes will fill up and the fish will get big so he can catch them.

Amy Loke

I wonder why each snowflake is different...

Small water droplets in a cloud may freeze, making tiny ice crystals. A snowflake is formed when these ice crystals join together. As more and more ice crystals join together, the snowflake gets heavier. Finally it starts falling to the earth. As the snowflake falls, more ice crystals may be added to it. There are many different kinds of ice crystals. Some are flat. Some are long. Some are pointy. Some are star-shaped. There are many ways that they can join together. Each combination makes a different kind of snowflake.

It has been said that no two snowflakes have ever been exactly alike. No one knows if this is really true, but there are certainly many different kinds of snowflakes.

Kathy Cox

I wonder how a gumball machine works...

The gumballs lie flat on a metal plate with holes in it. When you put a coin in and turn the handle, the metal plate goes around until a gumball goes through a hole in the metal plate and into your hand.

Crystal Joyce

I wonder why soap cleans...

Detergents and soaps clean by giving water more wetting power. The soap molecules surround the dirt particles on the item being cleaned, and pull the dirt out or off of the item and into the water and detergent particles so the dirt will not settle again on the item. The dirt is held in the water until it is rinsed away.

Lauren Campo

I wonder how cameras take pictures...

Cameras have a lens that is very much like our eyes. It opens up and lets light through. The light bounces off the film and the film copies what it sees. That's how a picture is made.

Josh Ellison

I wonder why a light bulb lights...

A light bulb glows because a wire inside gets hot when electricity surges through it. The wire is made from a special metal called tungsten. It is thinner than a hair from your head, and it is coiled like a spring. The thin coiled tungsten wire is called a filament.

Ben Garnett

I wonder how bikes move...

A long time ago, people moved their bikes by pushing against the ground with their feet. Then pedals were added. At first the pedals were attached to the front wheel. Then pedals were put in the center of the bike below the seat and connected to the back tire with a chain. When you move the pedals with your feet, the chain moves, and that moves the back tire which makes the bike move.

Steven Childers

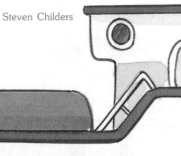

I wonder how big, heavy ships float in the water...

When an object weighs less than the amount of water taking up the same amount of space, the object floats. A big ship takes up a lot of space in water. Water in that much space would weigh even more than the ship, so the ship floats. If the ship had a hole in it, it would sink.

Michael Enos

I wonder why airplanes fly...

When I see them up close, I can't believe that airplanes can get off the ground. They are so big and heavy, it is hard to understand how the air can pick them up.

When airplanes travel on the ground at a very fast speed, the air above the wings moves faster than the air under the wings, causing the plane to lift off. Once it is in the air, the speed and airflow keep the airplane sailing. When it is time to land, the pilot must slow down. This is done with the flaps on the wings.

Now I know why airplanes fly.

Chris Betner

I wonder how a submarine goes under water...

A submarine has big tanks inside it. When the tanks are full of air, the submarine stays up. Sometimes the people on the submarine want to go down. Then they let water into the tanks. When water pushes the air out, the submarine goes down. When air is blown into the tanks, it pushes the water out and the submarine goes up.

Courtney Rusinko

I wonder why glue sticks...

Glue makes objects stick together by going through pores in their surfaces and then drying to form a hard bond. Glue is used for many, many things like toys and other things.

Kendra Peterson

I wonder why the hair on our heads keeps growing...

Hair grows by forming new cells at the root of each hair. As these new cells form, the old ones are pushed out of the openings in your scalp, called hair follicles, and die. As more cells die, your hair grows.

Brett Foley

I wonder why sweets make your teeth fall out...

Sweets attract bacteria. Bacteria causes cavities, which are holes in teeth. Cavities cause your teeth to rot, and this makes your teeth fall out. We brush our teeth to help stop sweets from making our teeth rot.

Chris Steude

I wonder why we can change the sound of our voices...

The larynx in your throat has strings like a musical instrument, called vocal cords. When you take in air, they vibrate and can make different sounds. When the strings are stretched tight, your voice sounds high and when the strings are loose, your voice sounds low.

Loni Zettle

I wonder why some people have curly hair while others have straight hair...

We all have holes in our scalps called follicles, which come in different shapes. Some are round. Some are oval. And some are narrow and long. If your hair is straight, your follicles are round. If your hair is a little curly, your follicles are oval. If your hair is very curly, your follicles are narrow and long. If you looked at your hair through a microscope, you would see that your type of hair matches your hair follicles. You cannot permanently change the type of hair you have. It will always stay the same.

Christy Williams

I wonder how people smell with their noses...

Your nose helps you smell. It can help you recognize danger. It can help you tell what flavor your bubble gum is. Also, it can help you smell breakfast. A nose is very important.

When you breathe, some of the air goes into your nose. There are special smell cells called receptor cells there. They send information about the smell to your brain. Your brain compares these smells with memories of other scents you've smelled before. That's how you know what you are smelling. All of this happens very quickly as you smell the many different scents in the air.

Catherine Coulter

I wonder why I have bones...

Bones give people shape. Bones store minerals, make blood cells, and help me grow straight. I think bones are important.

Megan McNeely

I wonder why my teeth fall out...

Baby teeth fall out to make room for adult teeth, which are bigger. As I grow bigger, my teeth need to change too. When I am 18, I will probably have all of my adult teeth.

Jon Hollingsworth

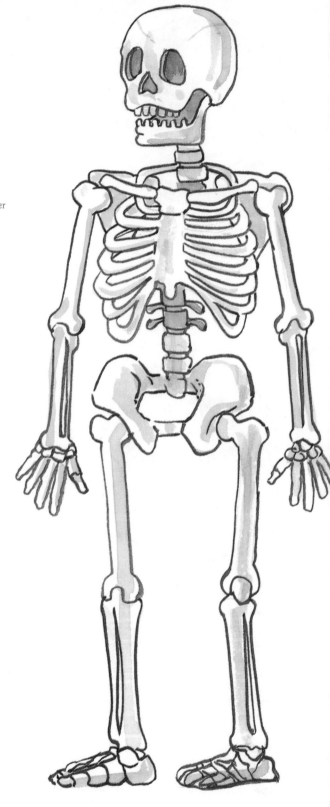

24

I wonder why I have a heart...

The heart pumps blood. The blood carries oxygen to the body. If we didn't have a heart, our blood wouldn't move at all and we couldn't live. Our heart is very important.

Nick Shadday

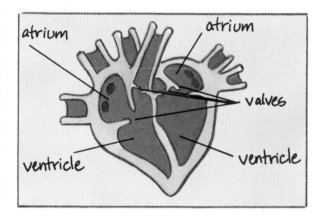

I wonder why my heart beats...

The heart beats because blood is being pumped through it. Your heart is a muscle and its openings are called valves. Your heart muscle squeezes and relaxes as the blood is pumped through the valves. Each squeeze and relaxation make up one beat of the heart.

Susan Doherty

I wonder why we need blood...

Blood is everywhere in your body. There are three important kinds of cells in your blood. They are red cells, white cells, and platelets.

Red cells are round and flat and thin in the middle, and they are so small you have to use a microscope to see them. There are millions of them in one drop of blood. They carry oxygen from your lungs and food from your intestines to every part of your body.

White cells are bigger than red cells. There are fewer white cells than red cells, but there are thousands of them in one drop of blood. White cells keep you from getting sick by eating disease germs.

Platelets are round and flat and clear. They gather at a cut to form a plug to stop the bleeding.

Kari Lynn Mazanec

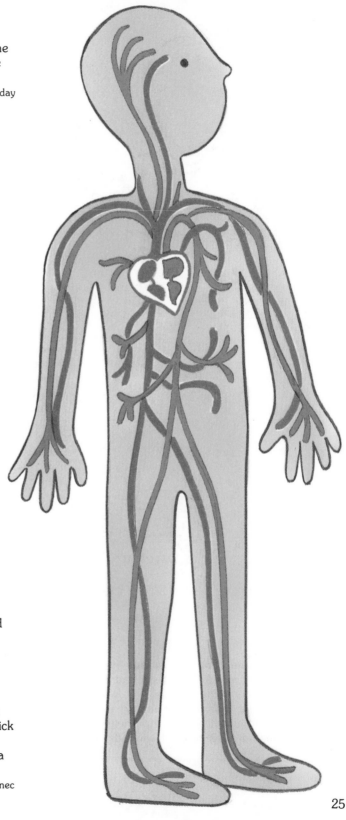

25

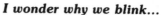

I wonder why we blink...

I think we blink because our eyes have been open too long and so we close them just a little bit and then open them again. When you blink, the water in your eye washes your eye so you can see better. The water in your eye also cleans out the dust in your eye. Your eyes stay clean because you blink.

Alice Lawler

I wonder why people have hair...

We have hair for protection from cold in the winter and for protection from the sun in the summer so our heads do not get sunburned.

Brandon Nicely

I wonder how freckles form...

Everyone has tiny grains of coloring called melanin in their skin. In some people, the melanin is gathered in little spots called freckles. Some people are born with freckles, others get freckles from being out on a nice, hot sunny day.

Susanne Smith

I wonder why we have wax in our ears...

Earwax is very useful. It allows sound to go in the ear but keeps everything else out. The wax hangs onto little tiny hairs in your ear and catches anything that shouldn't be there and helps keep it out. Too much earwax can block sounds.

Lauren Bodnar

I wonder why we sweat...

Your body is always working to keep you at the right temperature—98.6° F. When you play a lot or get hot, your body helps lower your temperature by making you sweat. As air blows on the sweat, you cool down.

Brad Yert

I wonder why people shiver when they are cold...

Shivering helps a person feel warmer. Your muscles tighten and relax very quickly over and over again. When your muscles work hard, you warm up.

Diane Williamson

I wonder why people get bruises...

When people bump a part of their body, it might turn blue or yellow the next day. This means small blood vessels in your body have been broken beneath the skin. When the blood goes out of these blood vessels, your skin turns blue or yellow. This is a bruise. When the blood vessels heal up, the bruise goes away.

David Perkins

I wonder why I sometimes get static electricity when I brush my hair...

If you brush your hair on a dry day, it will have static electricity because of a build-up of positive charges in your hair and negative charges built up in your comb.

Colleen McKenney

I wonder what our bodies are made of...

Our bodies are made of cells. Even our bones and teeth are made of cells. Most cells are so small that you can only see them under a microscope. Every part of our bodies is made of cells. Our bodies are made up of trillions and trillions of cells.

Brenna Mead

muscle cells

blood cells

skin cells

nerve cells

bone cells

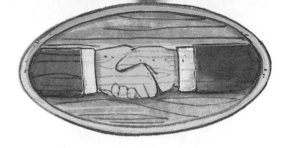

I wonder why people shake hands...

Long ago, European men would shake hands when they met as a way of saying "You can trust me." One man would hold out his hand to show the other that he was not going to pull out his sword. If the other man would hold out his hand too, then they would shake hands. Each man saw that the other man did not have a sword in his hand and they knew they could trust each other. Today we don't carry swords but shaking hands still means "You can trust me." Today, a handshake can mean "Hello," "Good-bye," "Welcome," "Nice to see you" or "I hope we meet again."

Sara Young

I wonder why we need gravity...

Gravity pulls and holds all things to the earth. Without gravity, we could not walk on the ground, sleep in bed or even throw a ball up in the air and expect it to come back down! Without gravity, we would float around in the air without ever landing. Our lives would be very different without gravity.

Courtney Hives

I wonder why the sun comes up...

The sun gives us light. The sun gives us heat. The sun can dry our clothes. The sun helps the plants grow. The sun tells us it's morning. The sun gives us pretty sunsets. Some people can tell time by looking at the sun. The sun ripens many fruits. The sun tans our skin. The sun recharges our brains.

Tyler Frakes

I wonder why we sneeze...

A sneeze works like a vacuum cleaner, only the other way around. It gets rid of any specks of dirt by blasting them out of your nose. Anything like dirt or chemicals that get into your nose can turn on the sneeze reflex. When the reflex starts, your brain makes you take a very deep breath. This happens during the "Ah-Ah-Ah" before the "Choo!" Air is quickly pushed up from the lungs and bursts out through your nose. The dirt gets carried out with the air.

Kacy Smith

I wonder why keys have bumps...

The bumps on a key will fit into the grooves and ridges of the lock they belong to and open it. Only the correct key has the correct pattern of bumps to fit into the grooves and ridges of the lock.

April Meyer

I wonder why the days of the week are named the way they are...

We call the first day of the week Sunday in honor of the sun. The second day of the week is Monday for the moon. The remaining days of the week are named for ancient gods. Tuesday is named for Tyr, the god of war. Wednesday is named for Woden. Thursday is named for Thor, the god of thunder. Friday is named for the goddess Frigg. Our name for Saturday comes from the Roman god Saturn.

Kristin Johnson

I wonder why your feet go to sleep...

A doubled-up leg is like a water hose with a kink in it. So when you sit with your leg crossed, the blood in your leg (like the water in the hose) cannot go through your leg easily. This is why your foot feels prickly.

Carter Hill

SUNDAY	MONDAY	TUESDAY	WEDNESDAY	THURSDAY	FRIDAY	SATURDAY
		1	2	3	4	5
6	7	8	9	10	11	12
13	14	15	16	17	18	19
20	21	22	23	24	25	26
27	28	29	30			

I wonder why we have commercials on television...

There are commercials on television because it costs so much to make a TV show. The cameras used to film a program cost a lot of money, and most shows use more than one camera. Plus the actors, directors and stage designers have to be paid. The electric bills for a television station are very high. Commercials are paid for by the company who makes the product being advertised. This is how television stations get money and why we can watch television programs for free.

Brandon Kiser

I wonder why we have rules...

We have rules because we need to have some kind of order. If we didn't have rules the world would be a mess. We follow rules to stay safe and in control. Rules set limits. Some people don't follow rules because they don't understand why rules are made. If everyone followed rules, the jails would be empty. If everyone followed rules, we wouldn't need police. Children should really follow rules in order to grow up safe and strong. Rules are necessary.

Michael Mack

I wonder why we yawn...

No one knows what causes us to yawn. You yawn when you are tired or bored. Sometimes you yawn just because someone nearby has yawned. Even reading about a yawn can make you yawn. When you exercise, you do not yawn, and you never yawn when you are angry or excited. Some yawns are probably caused by your body's need for extra oxygen. A big yawn brings extra oxygen into your body. But, the need for oxygen does not explain why yawns are contagious.

Jennifer Shefcuk

I wonder why a cactus plant has needles...

The desert is a difficult place for plants to live. The sun is very hot. The ground is very hard and dry. The cactus plant, however, knows how to survive there. When it rains, the cactus stores up all the water it can hold. The cactus needles protect the plant from being eaten by animals that want the water the plant stores inside. The needles also cast a shadow on the plant itself to protect it from the sun.

Chris Casper

I wonder why cactus plants don't need to be watered very much...

Cactus plants store water inside when it does rain, so they can go for a long time without needing to be watered. They just take water from their supply when they need it.

Whitney Green

I wonder why a Venus's-flytrap eats flies...

A Venus's-flytrap eats flies because it needs the special juice in the fly's body to grow. It gets some minerals from the soil, but some soils do not have nitrogen, which it needs to grow. Insects have the nitrogen that the plant needs for its diet.

The Venus's-flytrap catches insects with its leaves. It closes its leaves around the fly when it lands on it. The plant then changes the fly's flesh into a thick juice. It gets its food from this juice. After it is done with the fly, it opens its leaves and lets whatever is left blow away.

My mom gave her Venus's-flytrap a hamburger, and it ate it. Aren't these funny plants?

Greg Hoffman

I wonder why the ozone layer is important to us...

The ozone layer is a layer made up of a form of oxygen that is in the upper atmosphere called the stratosphere. This layer is important to us because it shields the earth from much of the sun's ultraviolet light. Ultraviolet rays harm living tissues. Without the ozone layer, plants and animals probably could not live on Earth.

Shaun Ferchak

I wonder why volcanoes erupt...

Volcanoes erupt when magma, which is found about 20 to 100 miles below the Earth's surface, gives off many gases. When the gases get very hot, they make a great amount of pressure and the magma pushes the gases to the Earth's surface. The magma and gases go to the weakest place on the surface, then explode.

Kelly Amburgey

I wonder why the Great Wall of China was built...

In the 200s B.C., the Emperor Shih Huangti had the wall built for protection from nomad warriors. The bottom of the wall is about 25 feet thick and the top is about 15 feet thick. It is 25 feet high and over 1,500 miles long.

Chris Sabin

I wonder what chocolate is made of...

Chocolate is made from the seeds of cacao trees. This tropical tree is found mainly on the west coast of Africa and in Brazil.

Nicole Ruehl

I wonder why some people wear green on St. Patrick's Day...

St. Patrick's Day is an Irish holiday. The Irish believe in a legend that says there are 40 shades of green in Ireland's landscape, where shamrocks grow wild and stay green all year long. They wear green to show they are Irish and believe in the legend.

Erin Kelly

I wonder where chalk comes from...

Chalk comes from millions of tiny animal shells which make up lime. When these animals die, their shells fall to the bottom of the water. Long ago, people found out that chalk is so soft that it can be used for writing. What fun to think we may be writing with the shells of little animals when we use chalk!

Lori Huber

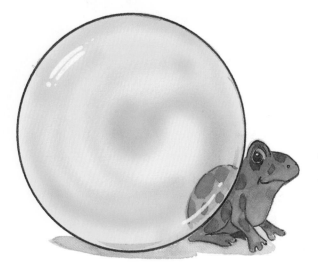

I wonder what marbles are made of...

Marbles are made of glass. A long time ago, they were made from clay or stone.

Jeri Cunningham

I wonder what "playing opossum" means...

It comes from the habit of the animal called an opossum. The opossum falls over and fakes being dead when danger is near, hoping the threat will leave it alone. "Playing opossum" means playing dead.

Corey Kritzman

I wonder why X means so many different things...

X is a letter in many alphabets. But it is also the number 10 in Roman numerals. X can stand for an amount that isn't known, or a word, or a name. It can also be a warning. X is the symbol for multiplication. X can mark a location on a map. An X sign above a highway tells you that a certain driving lane is closed. It can also tell you that a railroad crossing is ahead. X is used in the game of tic-tac-toe. And, as if these weren't enough things for X to mean, you can sign an X to stand for your name if you don't know how to write.

Shara Williams

I wonder why some people have freckles...

I have been told many reasons for my freckles, but I hate when people tell them to me. I hate it, for example, when they say, "The sun must have kissed you" or "The angels in heaven kissed you." I wonder if I was born with freckles. I wish I could get rid of my freckles. Maybe it's true that you get freckles from the sun because they fade in the winter and come back in the summer. People that have freckles must be special. I wonder why I have freckles. I wonder if I will always have freckles. Oh well, freckles aren't so bad after all, I guess.

Donald Pasco

I wonder why we have toes...

We have toes so that we can bump them into furniture in the dark, to test the temperature of the water in a swimming pool, and to sift through sand at the beach to find pieces of seashells.

Patrick Lindsey

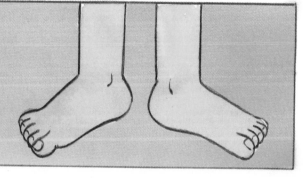

I wonder what sound is...

Sounds are vibrations that move through the air. When you clap your hands or stamp your feet, vibrations or sound waves travel out in big circles like ripples in a puddle when a stone is thrown into it. You have vocal cords in your throat that vibrate and make sounds when you talk or sing.

Beth Crow

I wonder why I cannot fly...

I wonder why I cannot fly.
If I could, I always would.
I'd go up high in the sky.
Just tell me why I cannot fly.
If I had wings, I'd do lots of things.
It's gravity that makes me too heavy.
If there wasn't any gravity,
All my friends would go up and fly with me.

Mel Ogg

I wonder why we get dizzy when we spin around...

Some people think that your ears only do one job—hear. But your ears also help you keep your balance. There is liquid in your ears and when you spin around, the liquid swirls around, too. The swirling liquid stimulates tiny hairs in your ears. The hairs send messages to the brain, telling it that you are spinning. Even after you stop spinning, the liquid still swirls around and tells your brain that you are still spinning. That's why you feel dizzy for a while after you stop spinning.

Erin Teeple

I wonder how crayons are made...

Crayons are made of wax and colored powder called pigments. There are a lot of different pigments, so we can get crayons in all different colors. Liquid wax and the pigments are mixed together in a huge vat, then poured into crayon molds. When the wax has hardened, you have crayons.

Edward Miller

I wonder why we have an alphabet...

Before we had letters to write with, people drew pictures to tell stories. Drawing pictures became too slow. So they abbreviated the pictures by creating symbols. These symbols became letters. Our alphabet came from the Roman alphabet, which came from the Greek alphabet. The Phoenicians developed the very first alphabet.

Kimee Langham

I wonder why some people's feet smell...

Bacteria and fungi live on people's feet. When your feet get dirty and you sweat, oil is produced on your skin. When this happens on your feet inside your shoes where it's dark, the fungi and bacteria grow. They feed on the dirt, sweat and oil. Then they produce that bad smell.

Justin Cade

I wonder why soda pop fizzes...

Soda contains carbonated water, which has little air bubbles in it. When you open a bottle or can of soda, the bubbles escape and make a "fizzing" sound.

Second Grade Class, Bradley Creek Elementary

I wonder why the sun rises in the east and sets in the west...

The earth is always spinning around. It takes the earth one day to turn all the way around. Then it starts over again. In the morning, the earth is at a certain point of its turn. If you look to the east while the earth is at this part of its turn, the sun looks like it is rising in the sky. At night, the earth is at the part of its turn that makes it look like the sun is going down in the west.

Tim Rexius

I wonder why stars twinkle...

Air makes stars appear to twinkle. In space, starlight does not twinkle. The light from the star passes through air to the earth. The air moves and changes, which makes the light from the stars blink.

Nick Jacobs

I wonder why the moon has craters...

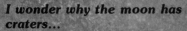

The moon has large craters because asteroids and comets hit its surface. Many are more than a mile wide, but the largest is about 700 miles across.

Nathan Deledda

I wonder why we can only see the stars at night...

The sun is closer to the earth than the other stars, and its light is so bright that we cannot see the light from the other stars in the daytime. The stars are still out there, of course. But the sun's light is many thousands of times brighter than starlight. The sun's light is spread out through the atmosphere, coloring it blue. In all this brightness, the light from the stars is lost.

Elizabeth Danner

I wonder why the moon shines...

The moon isn't a ball of hot, glowing gas like the sun. It's a ball of cold, hard rock. The moon does not actually give off light, it reflects it like a giant mirror. The light it sends to Earth is light that is reflected from the sun. The moon isn't a very good mirror, though. It isn't smooth and shiny. In fact, most of the rock on the moon is rough and dark gray. It doesn't really reflect much sunlight. But sunlight is so bright that even the tiny bit that is reflected from the moon makes the moon look like a glowing ball in our sky.

Brett Coron

I wonder why astronauts can float in space...

Because there is no gravity to hold them down in space.

Danielle Branch

I wonder why people travel to outer space...

We need to find out more information about what it is like to live in outer space. Maybe someday people will live in outer space and on other planets. Scientists are now trying to grow seeds in outer space.

Tiffany Buss

40

I wonder why people can live on Earth but not on Mercury...

People can't live on Mercury because it is the closest planet to the sun and it gets too hot. The temperature on Mercury is nearly 700° F during the day, but can drop to down to -300° F at night.

Melanie Pare

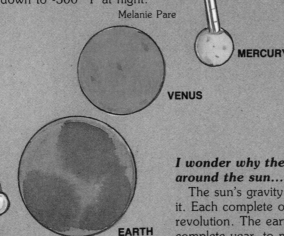

SUN

MERCURY

VENUS

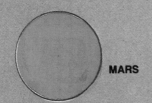

EARTH

I wonder why the earth revolves around the sun...

The sun's gravity forces the earth to orbit around it. Each complete orbit around the sun is called a revolution. The earth takes 365 days, or one complete year, to make one revolution around the sun.

Christy Marie Flanagan

MARS

I wonder why nobody lives on Mars...

I suppose nobody lives on Mars because there is no oxygen on Mars. You wouldn't be able to breathe up there, and you have to have oxygen to breathe and grow. All living things need air and water to live.

Cody Jones

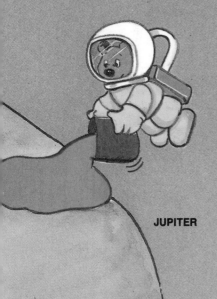

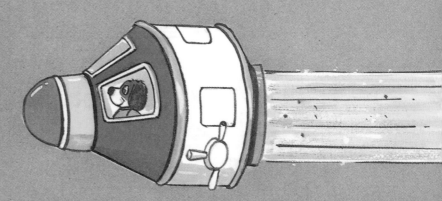

JUPITER

I wonder what the big red spot on Jupiter is...

Jupiter is the largest planet in our solar system. It is a bright planet and has a huge red spot on it called the Great Red Spot. The spot is really a huge storm that is over 300 years old.

Kyle Estes

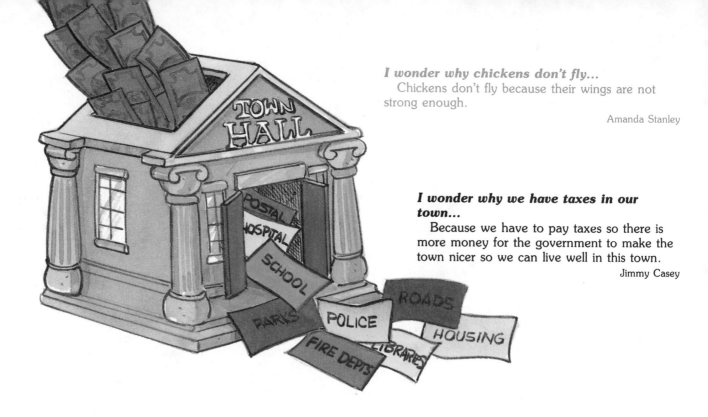

I wonder why chickens don't fly...

Chickens don't fly because their wings are not strong enough.

Amanda Stanley

I wonder why we have taxes in our town...

Because we have to pay taxes so there is more money for the government to make the town nicer so we can live well in this town.

Jimmy Casey

I wonder why fire stations used to have Dalmatians...

In the old days (before they had fire trucks), firefighters used horse-drawn carriages. Dalmatians walked next to the horses to make sure they stayed in line and went straight.

Courtney Alliston

I wonder why there can't be peace in the world...

Why can't all the people in the world get along? I guess it is because people believe in things that other people disagree with. People fight for things they believe in. But instead of talking things over, all they do is fight. The world would be a better place if people would try to get along with one another.

Nicholas Joles

I wonder why I go to school...

I go to school to learn math so that when I grow up I will know how to balance a checkbook. I will be able to count my change at the grocery store.

I also go to school to learn how to spell and read books. When I ride in the car, I can read the road signs from the window.

I learn about the community in school, and the many places to visit—the hospital, the post office, the bank, the grocery store, and more.

I learn so many things in school that I don't have to wonder anymore.

Natasha Hillman

I wonder how flying squirrels fly...

Flying squirrels can't really fly. They glide. Instead of wings, they have a piece of furry skin stretched between each front and back leg. This skin acts as a parachute when they go from tree to tree.

Jared Clark

44

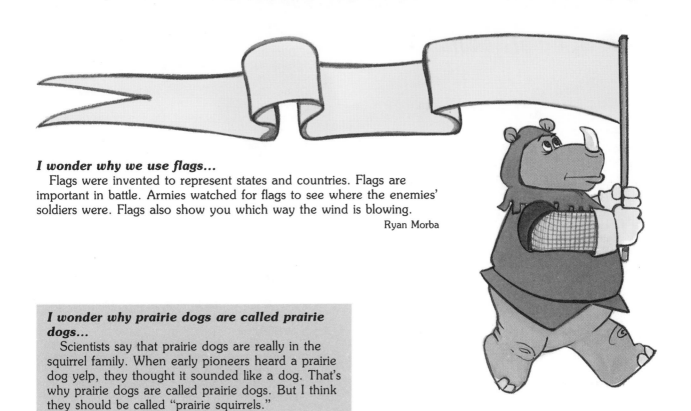

I wonder why we use flags...

Flags were invented to represent states and countries. Flags are important in battle. Armies watched for flags to see where the enemies' soldiers were. Flags also show you which way the wind is blowing.

Ryan Morba

I wonder why prairie dogs are called prairie dogs...

Scientists say that prairie dogs are really in the squirrel family. When early pioneers heard a prairie dog yelp, they thought it sounded like a dog. That's why prairie dogs are called prairie dogs. But I think they should be called "prairie squirrels."

Melissa Meyer

I wonder why I have to go to bed so early...

Different people need different amounts of sleep. Newborn babies need a lot of sleep to help them grow. Older people need less sleep. My baby sister needs more sleep than I do, but I need more than my dad. When I get older and bigger, I won't have to go to bed so early because my body won't need as much sleep and rest to grow.

Latron Tucker

A Special Thanks To:

Alliston, Courtney, Grade 3, Hillcrest Christian School, Jackson, MS

Amburgey, Kelly, Grade 2, New Egypt Elementary, New Egypt, NJ

Anderson, Krystal, Grade 2, Millington East Elementary, Millington, TN

Barber, Brooks, Grade 2, Bray Elementary, Cedar Hill, TX

Beattie, Meredith, Grade 3, Hillview Elementary, Idaho Falls, ID

Berry, Michael, Grade 2, Mission Glen Elementary, Houston, TX

Betner, Chris, Grade 2, Bethel Baptist Christian School, Cherry Hill, NJ

Bodnar, Lauren, Grade 3, Notre Dame Elementary, Chardon, OH

Bowman, Tiffany, 8, Farrington School, Augusta, ME

Branch, Danielle, Grade 2, Silverbrook School, Fairfax Station, VA

Bricker, Becky, Grade 2, Timothy Ball School, Crown Point, IN

Buss, Tiffany, Grade 2, Centennial School, Gresham, NE

Butler, David, Grade 3, Hillview Elementary, Idaho Falls, ID

Cade, Justin, 9, Charlotte Anderson Elementary, Arlington, TX

Callister, Kelly, Grade 3, Hillview Elementary, Idaho Falls, ID

Campo, Lauren, Grade 2, Mimosa Park Elementary, Luling, LA

Carter, Jessica, Grade 2, Lincoln Park Elementary, Knoxville, TN

Casey, Jimmy, Grade 2, Cyrus E. Dallin School, Arlington, MA

Casper, Chris, Grade 3, Vanstory Hills Elementary, Fayetteville, NC

Childers, Steven, Grade 2, Spring Garden Elementary, Bedford, TX

Clark, Jared, Grade 2, New Egypt Elementary, New Egypt, NJ

Coron, Brett, 8, Holy Rosary School, Flint, MI

Coulter, Catherine, Grade 2, Kemp Primary, Kemp, TX

Cox, Kathy, 8, Central Elementary, Corning, AR

Crow, Beth, Grade 2, Kemp Primary, Kemp, TX

Cunningham, Jeri, 7, Speegleville Elementary, Waco, TX

Danner, Elizabeth, Grade 2, Flint River Academy, Woodbury, GA

Dean, Jake, Grade 3, San Jose Elementary, Dunedin, FL

DelCorpo, Nicole, Grade 3, San Jose Elementary, Dunedin, FL

Deledda, Nathan, Grade 3, San Jose Elementary, Dunedin, FL

Demarchi, Nicky, Grade 3, San Jose Elementary, Dunedin, FL

DeWilfond, Nicole, Grade 2, Riverdale Elementary, Port Byron, IL

Dixon, Chris, Grade 3, Windermere School, Ellington, CT

Doherty, Susan, Grade 2, University Lab School, Baton Rouge, LA

Douin, Joshua, 9, Farrington School, Augusta, ME

Ellison, Josh, Grade 2, Chapin Elementary, Chapin, SC

Engel, Stephen, Grade 2, Kinloch School, Dearborn Heights, MI

Enos, Michael, Grade 3, Fairmont Catholic School, Fairmont, WV

Estes, Kyle, Grade 2, Flint River Academy, Woodbury, GA

Ferchak, Shaun, Grade 3, Park School, Munhall, PA

Flanagan, Christy Marie, Grade 3, W.B. Redding School, Lizella, GA

Foley, Brett, Grade 3, Park School, Munhall, PA

Frakes, Tyler, Grade 2, Lewis & Clark School, Godfrey, IL

Gahhos, Rosanna, 8, Garden Elementary, Venice, FL

Gammon, Amy, Grade 2, University Lab School, Baton Rouge, LA

Garnett, Ben, Grade 2, Irving School, Joplin, MO

Garstecki, Katie, Grade 3, Saint Hugo of the Hills School, Bloomfield Hills, MI

Godfrey, Sean, Grade 2, Mission Glen Elementary, Houston, TX

Gray, Allison, Grade 3, Pendleton St. School, Brewer, ME

Green, Whitney, Grade 3, Academy Elementary, Temple, TX

Grosserode, Heather, Grade 3, Sacred Heart School, Norfolk, NE

Hall, Jacob, Grade 2, Lewis & Clark School, Godfrey, IL

Higham, Jenny, Grade 3, Hillview Elementary, Idaho Falls, ID

Hill, Carter, Grade 2, University Lab School, Baton Rouge, LA

Hillman, Natasha, Grade 2, E.L. Ficquett Elementary, Covington, GA

Hives, Courtney, Grade 2, University Lab School, Baton Rouge, LA

Hoffman, Greg, Grade 2, Bethel Baptist Christian School, Cherry Hill, NJ

Hollingsworth, Jon, Grade 2, Chapin Elementary, Chapin, SC

Huber, Lori, Grade 3, San Jose Elementary, Dunedin, FL

Hunter, Julie, Grade 3, San Jose Elementary, Dunedin, FL

Indra, Beth, Grade 3, Sacred Heart School, Norfolk, NE

Jacobs, Nick, Grade 2, Lewis & Clark School, Godfrey, IL

Jennings, Marianne, Grade 3, St. Pascal School, Chicago, IL

Johnson, Kristin, Grade 2, Vineland Elementary, Rotunda West, FL

Joles, Nicholas, 8, Charlotte Anderson Elementary, Arlington, TX

Jones, Cody, 6, Our Lady Star of the Sea School, New Orleans, LA

Joyce, Crystal, Grade 3, Lakehill School, Dallas, TX

Kankey, Ben, Grade 2, Bismarck Elementary, Bismarck, MO

Kelly, Erin, Grade 3, Rupert Elementary, Pottstown, PA

Kiser, Brandon, Grade 2, Bourbon Central Elementary, Paris, KY

Kois, Matthew, Grade 2, P.S. 52, Brooklyn, NY

Kritzman, Corey, Grade 3, Lt. Peter Hansen School, Canton, MA

Lake, Shauntelle, Grade 3, Windermere School, Ellington, CT

Langham, Kimee, 8, Garden Elementary, Venice, FL

Lawler, Alice, Grade 3, Highlands Elementary, Cedar Hill, TX

Lindsey, Patrick, Grade 2, Heritage Academy, Bakersfield, CA

Lindstrom, Fairreia, Grade 2, Mt. Sterling Elementary, Mt. Sterling, KY

Loke, Amy, Grade 2, Bray Elementary, Cedar Hill, TX

Mack, Michael, Grade 3, San Jose Elementary, Dunedin, FL

Marin, Sarah, Grade 2, Lewis & Clark School, Godfrey, IL

Mata, Jennifer, Grade 3, Crestview South Elementary, Wren, OH

Mathews, Amy, Grade 2, New Egypt Elementary, New Egypt, NJ

Mazanec, Kari Lynn, Grade 3, Notre Dame Elementary, Chardon, OH

McArthur, Melissa, Grade 3, Purdy Elementary, Purdy, MO

McKenney, Colleen, Grade 2, Vineland Elementary, Rotunda West, FL

McNeely, Megan, Grade 2, Chapin Elementary, Chapin, SC

Mead, Brenna, Grade 3, Windermere School, Ellington, CT

Merriman, James, Grade 3, Hillcrest Christian School, Jackson, MS

Meyer, April, Grade 3, Hillcrest Christian School, Jackson, MS

Meyer, Christy, Grade 3, Morgan County R-2 Schools, Versailles, MO

Meyer, Melissa, Grade 3, San Jose Elementary, Dunedin, FL

Miller, Edward, Grade 3, Park School, Munhall, PA

Morba, Ryan, Grade 3, Rupert Elementary, Pottstown, PA

Mutter, Ashley, Grade 3, Rupert Elementary, Pottstown, PA

Nicely, Brandon, Grade 2, Bradenville School, Bradenville, PA

Ogg, Mel, Grade 2, Russell School, Broomall, PA

Ondo, Paul, Grade 3, Park School, Munhall, PA

Overton, Edward, Grade 2, University Lab School, Baton Rouge, LA

Pantano, Brooke, Grade 3, Highlands Elementary, Cedar Hill, TX

Pare, Melanie, 8, Farrington School, Augusta, ME

Pasco, Donald, Grade 3, Lincoln Park Elementary, Muskegon, MI

Perkins, David, Grade 2, Erskine Elementary, Cedar Rapids, IA

Peterson, Kendra, Grade 3, Pendleton St. School, Brewer, ME

Rexius, Tim, Grade 3, Sacred Heart School, Norfolk, NE

Richardson, Sally, Grade 2, L.S.U. Lab School, Baton Rouge, LA

Ricks, Stephen, Grade 2, Lewis & Clark School, Godfrey, IL

Rivera, Daniel, Grade 2, P.S. 52, Brooklyn, NY

Ruehl, Nicole, Grade 2, Timothy Ball School, Crown Point, IN

Rusinko, Courtney, Grade 3, West Point School, Greensburg, PA

Sabin, Chris, Grade 3, San Jose Elementary, Dunedin, FL

Sawyer, Lindsay, Grade 3, San Jose Elementary, Dunedin, FL

Schroer, Robin, Grade 2, Vineland Elementary, Rotunda West, FL

Seaman, Aaron, Grade 2, Little Flower School, Sioux Falls, SD

Second Grade Class, Bradley Creek Elementary, Wilmington, NC

Shadday, Nick, Grade 2, Chapin Elementary, Chapin, SC

Shaffer, Marianne, Grade 3, San Jose Elementary, Dunedin, FL

Shefcuk, Jennifer, Grade 3, Notre Dame Elementary, Chardon, OH

Smith, Kacy, Grade 2, P.S. 52, Brooklyn, NY

Smith, Susanne, 7, South Euless Elementary, Euless, TX

Stanley, Amanda, Grade 2, Cumberland Elementary, Cumberland, VA

Stephens, Angel, Grade 2, Lewis & Clark School, Godfrey, IL

Steude, Chris, Grade 2, Chapin Elementary, Chapin, SC

Stringfield, Teressa, Grade 2, Bethel Baptist Christian School, Cherry Hill, NJ

Teeple, Erin, Grade 3, North Rose Elementary, North Rose, NY

Toth, Jessica, Grade 3, San Jose Elementary, Dunedin, FL

Toth, Pamela, 7, Garden Elementary, Venice, FL

Tucker, Latron, Grade 2, Chapin Elementary, Chapin, SC

Vanerelli, Andrea Rerea, Grade 3, West Oxford School, Oxford, NC

Weiss, Jerod, Grade 3, Kewaskum Elementary, Kewaskum, WI

Westphahl, Rachel, Grade 3, Gracemor Elementary, Kansas City, MO

Wheeler, Adam, 8, Central Elementary, Corning, AR

Whidden, Eric, Grade 3, Windermere School, Ellington, CT

Williams, Christy, Grade 2, ''Greenwood'' at W.B. Wicker School, Sanford, NC

Williams, Shara, Grade 3, Mercer School, Princeton, WV

Williamson, Diane, 8, Bon Meade School, Coraopolis, PA

Yert, Brad, Grade 3, Notre Dame Elementary, Chardon, OH

Young, Sara, Grade 2, Lewis & Clark School, Godfrey, IL

Zettle, Loni, Grade 3, Sugar Valley School, Loganton, PA